The 100 Deadliest Karate Moves

The 100 Deadliest Karate Moves

by
Dr. Ted Gambordella,
5th Dan

Paladin Press
Boulder, Colorado

Also by Dr. Ted Gambordella:

The Complete Book of Karate Weapons
Fight for Your Life! The Secrets of Street Fighting

The 100 Deadliest Karate Moves
by Ted Gambordella
Copyright © 1982 by Ted Gambordella

ISBN 0-87364-245-7
Printed in the United States of America

Published by Paladin Press, a division of
Paladin Enterprises, Inc., P.O. Box 1307,
Boulder, Colorado 80306, USA.
(303) 443-7250

Direct inquiries and/or orders to the above address.

Dedicated to the memory of
DEMETRIUS HAVANUS (The Golden Greek).
I have lost a good friend, and the arts have
lost a great teacher and fighter.
We will all miss you, very much.

Warning

The techniques in this book are aggressive and violent methods that are *not* meant for self-defense. Likewise, this book is *not* a training manual. It is offered *for information purposes only*. Neither the author nor the publisher assumes any responsibility for the use or misuse of the information contained herein.

Contents

Introduction

I wrote *The 100 Deadliest Karate Moves* as a practical text for the serious martial arts student or teacher. It is solely meant to be used as a reference in practice, and I do not condone or suggest that any of the techniques found in this book be used in the street against another man, unless, of course, the defender's life is in immediate danger. The techniques found in this book were not devised by me, and most are common knowledge to the average student.

What I have attempted to do is to compile moves in such a manner that one can study the kicks and blows and then can see the exact technique and target area, with the resulting damage to the attacker. I am assuming that the reader will have an adequate martial arts background so that he knows the basic stances and strikes. Therefore, I am showing only the strike or kick to the target area, without reference to body stances or other basics. All blows and kicks must be delivered with the utmost speed and power in order to be effective.

In a final chapter I show examples of street applications of some of the techniques. This is meant as a training section in order to get the student or teacher to begin to think of how the strikes and blows might be applied in a life-or-death situation.

If you study this book and practice the techniques until you are a master of them, you can become one of the most deadly men or women in the world.

1. Kicking Techniques

The most powerful techniques of karate are the kicking techniques. They are beautiful to watch and devastating in their results. When done by a martial artist who has adequate flexibility, control, speed, and power, kicks are unstoppable and almost unbelievably powerful. A black belt is quite capable of kicking through 3 to 5 inches of wood, or stomping through several inches of concrete. The effect of such power on a human target is usually crippling, and it almost certainly will stop any fight from continuing.

All kicks must be done with proper form, balance, speed, control, accuracy, and, of course, power. These attributes usually come after many years of hard training. It is not my intention in this book to teach you fundamentals; the information here is intended for use by a martial artist with years or at least many months of hard training both on his/her own and in the dojo with a competent teacher. I will, however, demonstrate the correct form for each kick, and then we will take the kicks and use them in attacks on the body's various vital points in *Chapter 2*. These vital points are anatomical areas where a minimum amount of force will produce maximum damage. Caution must be exercised when practicing these deadly moves, since it is all too easy to cripple or even kill your opponent with them.

BASIC STRIKES

The Front Snap Kick

Lift the knee of the kicking leg as high as possible in front of the body, be sure to keep the fists tight, and the toes turned upward to prevent damage to the foot.

Snap the kick out directly in front of the body to the target area, keep the other leg slightly bent for balance, and be sure to thrust with the hips for speed and power.

The Front Heel Thrust

This kick is similar to the front snap, but uses the heel for the striking area, and it has more power and penetration. The kicking technique is the same. However, you thrust more directly forward with this kick, and be sure to lock the leg for the full power to the heel.

The Front Snap—High

This kick requires a lot of flexibility and balance if any power is to be produced. It is extremely effective for areas of the face, throat, and chin.

The Side Kick

This is one of the most powerful kicks and is used for most areas of the body. Lift the kicking leg as high as possible to the front of the body, curling the toes of the foot inward for protection.

Snap, and thrust the kick directly to the side and the target area; be sure to snap the hips into the kick for full power. The heel, or side of the heel, is the striking area. Keep the arm above the leg, down the side of your body to protect your ribs.

The Roundhouse Kick

This is one of the fastest and most precise kicks. Lift the leg as high as possible to the front of the body, much like the beginning of a front kick. *Note*: we will be doing the roundhouse from the front foot, not the back, for more speed and power.

side view

front view
(high kick)

Snap the kick directly around the body to the striking area, keep the leg level the entire kick, and do not drop the knee down. Be sure to curl the toes back to protect them from being broken.

The Back Kick

This is probably the most devasting kick and the hardest to stop when done correctly. Bring the leg up about hip high, directly in front of the body. Look behind over your shoulder to the target area.

Thrust directly back with speed and power, snapping the hips for more power, and strike the heel of the foot into the desired area.

The Stomp

This kick is used when the attacker is already on the ground, due to a previous kick or punch. Raise the leg to about the hip, curl the toes up, and aim the heel down to the striking area.

Thrust directly down with the heel into the target area, smashing the heel as hard as possible into the target and trying to keep the leg straight for more power. *Note:* you must train your heel to withstand an extreme impact, or you will bruise it during this kick. You may train you foot with a makawara board, or on trees, etc.

The Knee

This kick is used when the attacker is too close to use an extension kick and is quite capable of stopping the largest of men. Raise the knee directly up with power and speed to the striking area. You get more power by thrusting or snapping up with the hips on this kick.

2. Vital Points & Kick Attacks

All of the kicks demonstrated in this section will do permanent damage to an attacker's body, if done with appropriate speed, power, and accuracy. We are shown demonstrating the vital points and the best kick attack for each one. Beneath the illustration, you will find the damage and the results that you can expect from using each kick against a would-be attacker.

One: Front Snap to the Shin

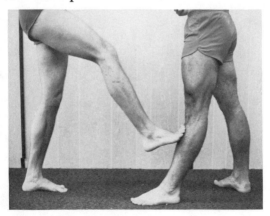

Damage: broken shin, bruised shin.
Result: attacker unable to stand or to continue to fight.

Two: Front Heel Kick to Shin

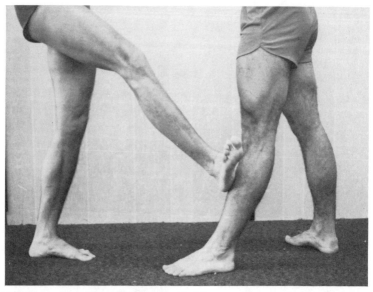

Damage: broken shin, bruised shin.
Result: attacker unable to stand or to continue fight.

Three: Front Snap to Kneecap

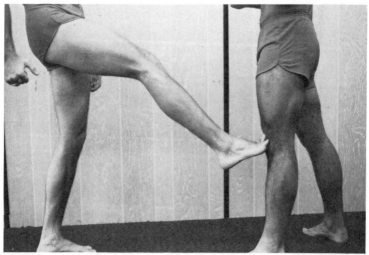

Damage: dislocated knee, broken kneecap, sprained, torn ligaments, tendons.
Result: attacker unable to stand or to continue fight; will require surgery to correct.

Four: Front Heel Kick Across Kneecap

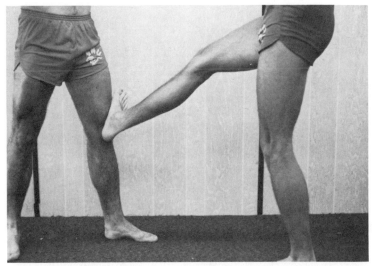

Damage: dislocated knee, broken kneecap, torn tendons and ligaments.
Result: attacker unable to stand or to continue to fight; will require surgery to correct.

Five: Front Snap to Coccyx (Tailbone)

Damage: broken coccyx, extreme pain.
Result: attacker unable to stand or to sit, will require medical attention.

Six: Front Snap to Lower Back

Damage: broken back, bruised kidneys, extreme pain.
Result: attacker may be permanently crippled; requires medical attention immediately.

Seven: Front Snap to Ribs

Damage: broken ribs, bruised lungs, extreme pain, loss of breath.
Result: attacker will be unable to breathe for several minutes; will fall down.

Eight: Front Snap with Heel to Chin

Damage: broken jaw, crushed jaw, teeth knocked out, loss of consciousness.
Result: attacker will be knocked out for several minutes.

Nine: Front Snap to Throat

Damage: crushed throat, smashed Adam's apple.
Result: attacker will die, usually, unless given immediate medical attention.

Ten: Front Snap to Solar Plexus

Damage: broken or bruised ribs, loss of breath, extreme pain.
Result: attacker will be unable to breathe for several minutes.

Eleven: Front Snap with Heel to Pelvis

Damage: crushed testicles, broken pelvis, internal damage to groin area.
Result: attacker will be unable to stand and may suffer permanent, crippling injury.

Twelve: Front Snap with Shin Area to Testicles

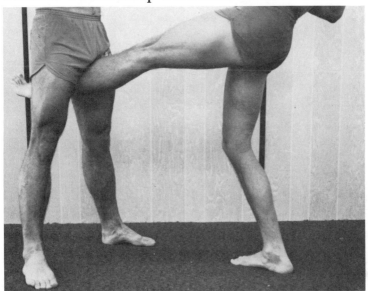

Damage: crushed testicles, cracked pelvis.
Result: attacker will be unable to stand; will usually require surgery, and often will be permanently crippled.

Thirteen: Side Kick to Knee

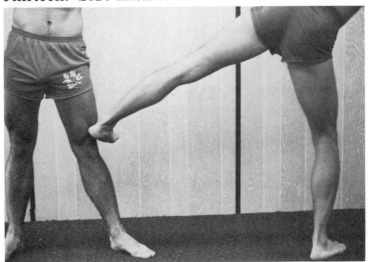

Damage: dislocated knee, torn ligaments and tendons.
Result: attacker will be unable to stand or to continue to fight; will require surgery to correct knee.

Fourteen: Side Snap Kick to Ribs

Damage: broken ribs, possible lung damage, internal damage.
Result: attacker will be unable to stand or to breathe for several minutes.

Fifteen: Side Kick to Throat

Damage: crushed throat, broken Adam's apple.
Result: attacker will die unless given immediate medical attention.

Sixteen: Side Kick to Jaw

Damage: broken jaw, teeth knocked out, loss of consciousness.

Result: attacker will be knocked out for several minutes, require medical attention.

Seventeen: Side Kick to Face

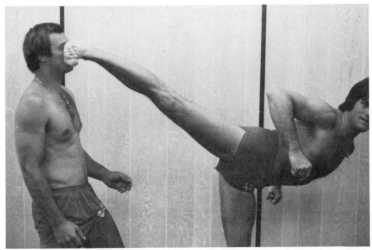

Damage: broken nose, teeth knocked out, broken jaw, loss of consciousness.

Result: attacker will be knocked out for several minutes.

Eighteen: Side Kick to Chin

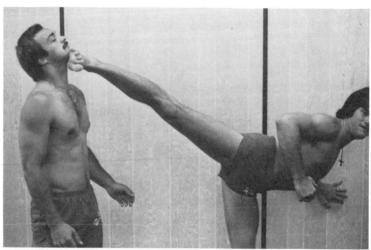

Damage: broken jaw, teeth knocked out, loss of consciousness.

Result: attacker will be knocked out for several minutes.

Nineteen: Side Kick to Heart

Damage: crushed or cracked chest, broken sternum, possibly stopped heart.

Result: attacker will be unable to breathe for several minutes; may die.

Twenty: Side Kick to Back of Head

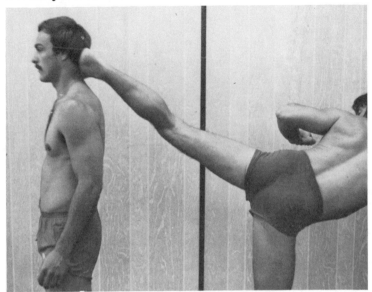

Damage: broken neck, loss of consciousness.
Result: attacker will be knocked out, usually permanently crippled; may die.

Twenty-One: Roundhouse Kick to Kidneys

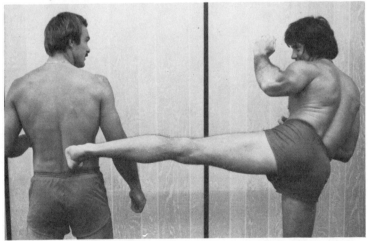

Damage: bruised kidneys, possibly broken back, extreme pain.
Result: attacker will usually fall down, have internal damage, and be in pain for weeks.

Twenty-Two: Roundhouse to Side of Head

Damage: broken jaw, teeth knocked out, eardrum busted, loss of consciousness.

Result: attacker will pass out, lose balance and ability to fight.

Twenty-Three: Roundhouse to Temple (toes directly contact temple)

Damage: cracked skull, nerve damage, blood stoppage to brain.

Result: attacker will be knocked out, may go into a fit or delirium.

Twenty-Four: Roundhouse to Side of Neck

Damage: bruised or broken neck, extreme pain, loss of blood to brain.
Result: attacker will pass out for several minutes.

Twenty-Five: Roundhouse to Solar Plexus

Damage: cracked or broken ribs, loss of breath, possible internal damage.
Result: attacker will be unable to stand or breathe for several minutes.

Twenty-Six: Roundhouse to Knee

Damage: broken knee, torn and sprained ligaments and tendons.

Result: attacker will be unable to stand or to continue to fight.

Twenty-Seven: Roundhouse to Groin

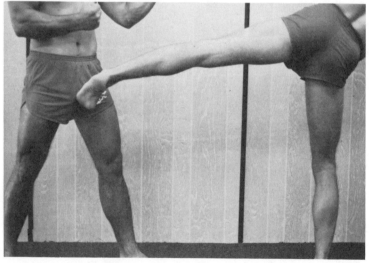

Damage: crushed testicles, broken or cracked pelvis.

Result: attacker will be unable to stand and will be in great pain, maybe crippled.

Twenty-Eight: Knee to Groin

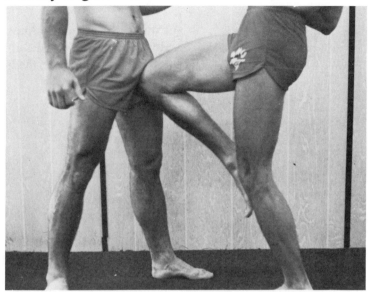

Damage: crushed testicies, cracked pelvis.
Result: attacker will be unable to stand, will be in great pain,
and possibly permanently crippled.

Twenty-Nine: Knee to Face

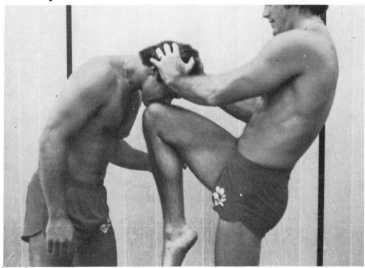

Damage: broken nose, cracked teeth, broken jaw.
Result: attacker will be knocked out for several minutes.

Thirty: Knee to Throat

Damage: crushed windpipe.
Result: attacker will die unless given immediate medical attention.

Thirty-One: Knee to Coccyx

Damage: broken or cracked
coccyx.
Result: attacker will be unable to stand or to sit, will
require medical attention.

Thirty-Two: Knee to Kidney and Lower Back

Damage: broken lower back.
Results: attacker will be in
great pain and have internal
damage requiring a doctor.

Thirty-Three: Knee Drop to Heart

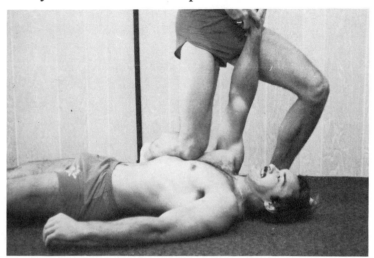

Damage: heart will be stopped, rib cage crushed, lungs punctured.
Result: attacker will usually die unless given immediate medical help.

Thirty-Four: Stomp to Heart

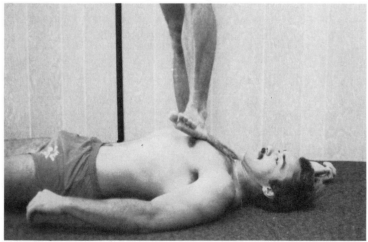

Damage: stopped heart, cracked or crushed chest, punctured lungs.
Result: attacker will usually die unless given immediate medical attention.

Thirty-Five: Stomp to Groin

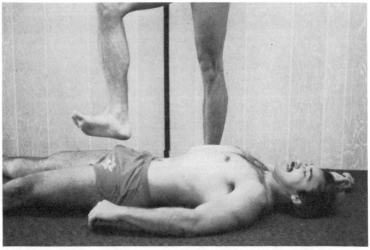

Damage: crushed groin, cracked pelvis.
Result: attacker will be unable to stand, may be crippled.

Thirty-Six: Stomp to Throat

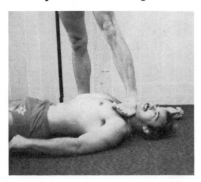

Damage: crushed throat.
Result: attacker will usually die unless given immediate medical attention.

Thirty-Seven: Stomp to Face

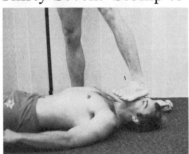

Damage: broken nose, broken jaw, teeth knocked out.
Result: attacker will remain unconscious for several minutes; require surgery.

Thirty-Eight: Stomp to Back of Head

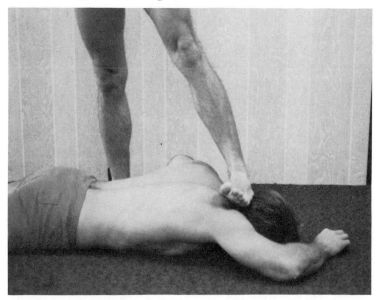

Damage: teeth knocked out, neck broken, concussion.
Result: permanent crippling, broken neck may cause death.

Thirty-Nine: Stomp to Lower Back

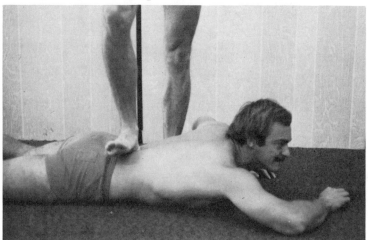

Damage: broken back, cracked vertebrae, internal damage.
Result: attacker will be unable to stand; may be permanently crippled.

Forty: Stomp to Coccyx

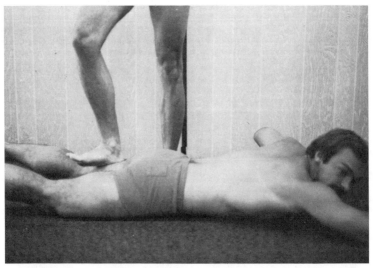

Damage: broken or cracked coccyx.
Result: attacker will be unable to stand or to sit for weeks.

Forty-One: Heel Kick to Top of Head

Damage: cracked skull, teeth broken.
Result: loss of consciousness for several minutes.

Forty-Two: Heel Kick to Temple

Damage: crushed temple, cracked skull, blood stoppage to brain.
Result: attacker will pass out for several minutes or go into a fit.

Forty-Three: Heel Kick to Back of Head

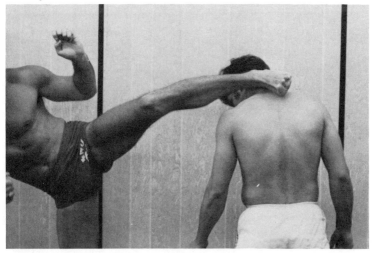

Damage: broken neck, loss of consciousness, broken jaw.
Result: attacker will pass out for several minutes; may be permanently crippled.

Forty-Four: Heel Kick to Throat

Damage: crushed throat.
Result: attacker will usually die unless given immediate medical help.

Forty-Five: Heel Kick to Face

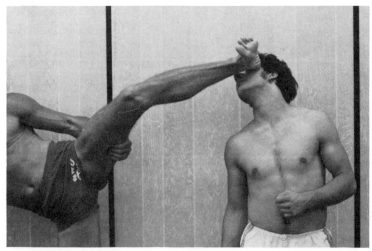

Damage: broken nose, teeth knocked out, jaw broken.
Result: attacker will be knocked out for several minutes, require medical help.

Forty-Six: Front Knee Strangle

Damage: loss of breath.
Result: death, unless pressure is released.

Forty-Seven: Leg Strangle

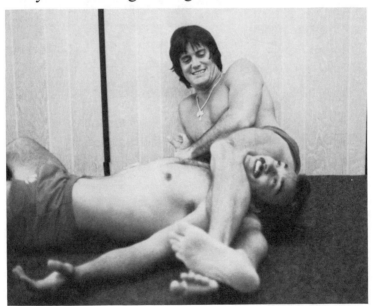

Damage: loss of breath.
Result: death, unless pressure is released.

3. Hand Techniques

The use of the hands in karate cannot be overemphasized. They are deadly in their speed and accuracy and can be devastatingly powerful when used by a skilled practitioner of the martial arts. Speed, power, accuracy, and technique are essential for effective results, and these attributes usually come only after years of training, both on your own and with a competent teacher.

The use of a makawara board and a heavy bag for toughening the hands and wrists is highly recommended, along with weight training for upper body strength. I am assuming that you already have your basic stances and movements down, so we will not discuss them here, except to mention that these basics take years to learn.

We will first demonstrate the basic hand attack techniques in this chapter. In the following chapter, we will then demonstrate how to use these hand attacks against the body's vital points, in the most efficient and deadly manner possible.

BASIC STRIKES

Shuto—Knife Hand

Hold the fingers of the hand tightly together and curl the thumb down. Strike with the edge of the hand onto the target area.

Palm Heel

Curl the fingers back tightly and the thumb is bent in. Strike with the palm area of the hand.

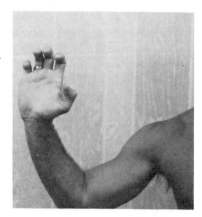

Two-Finger Eye Strike

Curl the fingers of the hand back and hold the other fingers securely with the thumb to keep them out of the way.

Thumb Gouge

Curl the fingers tightly into a fist, and extend the thumb out to the side for striking or gouging.

Foreknuckle Punch (basic karate punch)

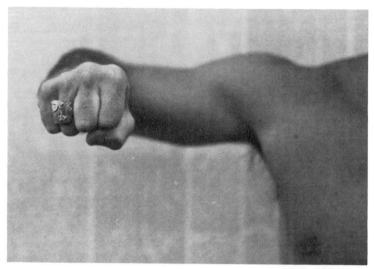

Make a tight fist with the fingers, rolling the thumb over the bottom of the hand and on top of the fingers. Strike with the first two knuckles to target areas.

Bottom Fist

Make a tight fist and you will notice a large ball of muscle form on the side of the hand; use this ball for striking the targets.

Ridge Hand

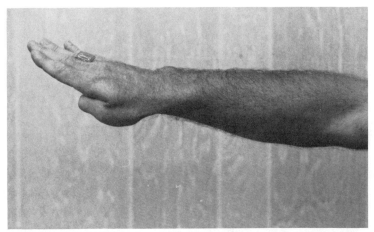

Curl the thumb back and hold it tightly against the palm. Keep the fingers straight, strike with the inside of the hand to target areas.

Elbow

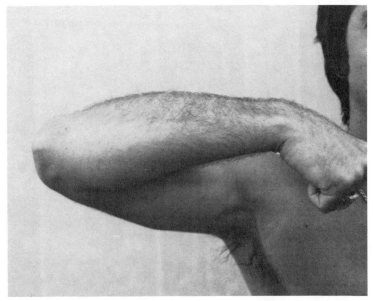

Bend the arm and use the point of the elbow for striking target areas.

4. Vital Points & Hand Attacks

If the following hand attacks are used in defensive situations, they can inflict serious damage upon an attacker when the hand technique is applied with the necessary speed, power, and accuracy. The vital points and appropriate attacks to each area are illustrated, with a notation on the damage and results of each hand attack.

Forty-Eight: Shuto to the Throat

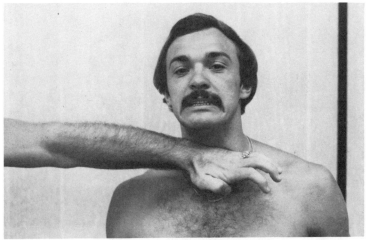

Damage: crushed throat, broken Adam's apple.
Result: attacker will usually die unless given immediate medical help.

41

Forty-Nine: Shuto to Teeth

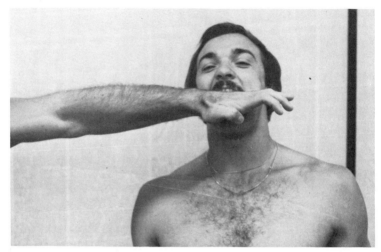

Damage: teeth knocked out, jaw broken.
Result: attacker will usually be knocked out or unwilling to continue to fight.

Fifty: Shuto to Eyes, Bridge of Nose

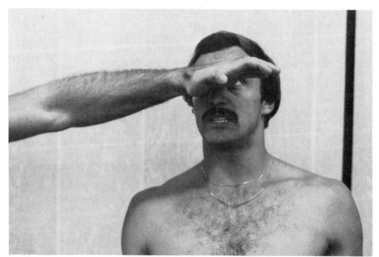

Damage: broken nose, loss of vision, concussion.
Result: attacker will be knocked out for several minutes.

Fifty-One: Shuto to Top of Skull

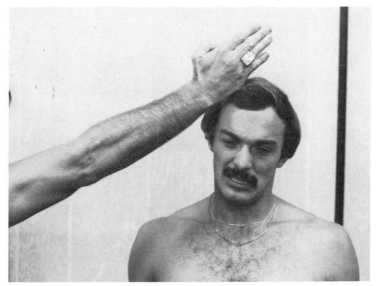

Damage: broken or cracked skull, concussion.
Result: attacker will be knocked out for several minutes.

Fifty-Two: Shuto to Solar Plexus

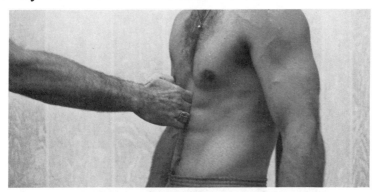

Note: This can be done in traditional shuto style, open hand or as I am doing here with closed fingers, or forefinger strike. This gives more power and deeper penetration, but if your fingers are weak, use the regular shuto.
Damage: breath knocked out, loss of consciousness, extreme pain.
Result: attacker will be unable to move, breathe, and will be unable to finish attack.

Fifty-Three: Shuto to Collarbone

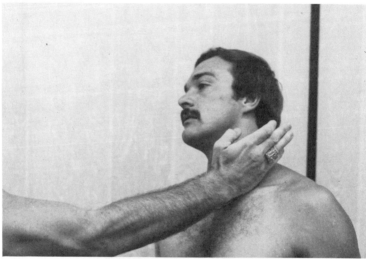

Damage: broken collarbone.
Result: attacker will be unable to pick up arm or to continue to fight.

Fifty-Four: Shuto to Side of Neck

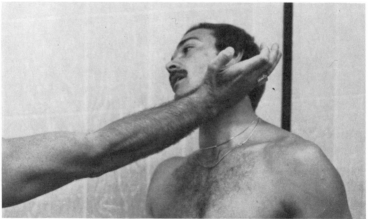

Damage: broken neck, loss of blood to brain.
Result: attacker will be knocked out for several seconds, or minutes.

Fifty-Five: Shuto to Jaw, Side of Face

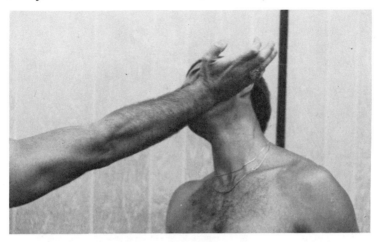

Damage: broken jaw, teeth knocked out.
Result: attacker will lose consciousness for several minutes.

Fifty-Six: Shuto to Ribs

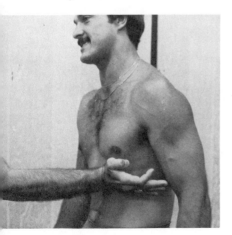

Damage: broken ribs, possible lung damage.
Result: attacker will be unable to breathe for several minutes.

Fifty-Seven: Shuto to Groin

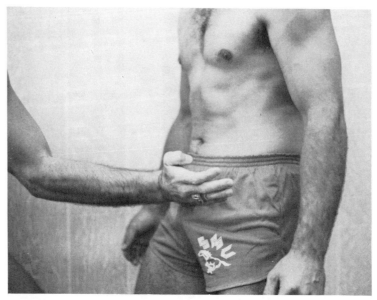

Damage: cracked pelvis, crushed groin area.
Result: attacker will be in great pain, unable to stand, may be crippled.

Fifty-Eight: Shuto to Back of Neck

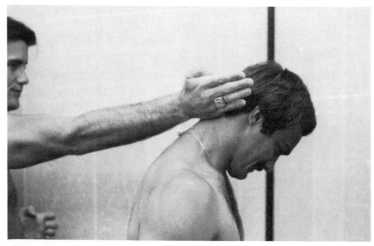

Damage: broken neck.
Result: permanent crippling, possible death.

Fifty-Nine: Shuto to Temple

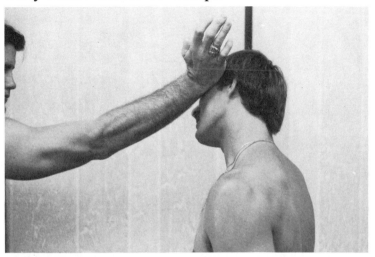

Damage: cracked skull, loss of consciousness, crushed temple. Result: attacker will be knocked out, or go into a fit or delirium.

Sixty: Shuto to Kidneys

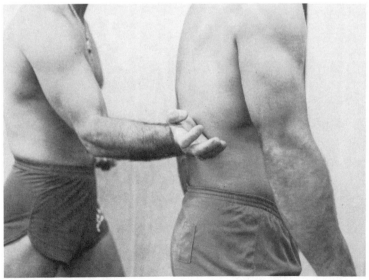

Damage: bruised kidneys, cracked or bruised ribs, great pain. Result: attacker will suffer internal damage and be in great pain.

Sixty-One: Palm Heel to Face

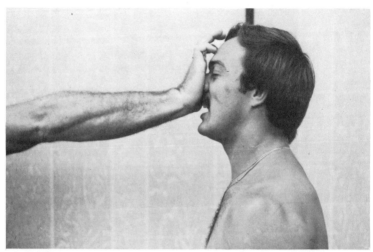

Damage: broken nose, teeth knocked out, broken jaw.
Result: attacker will be knocked out for several minutes.

Sixty-Two: Palm Heel to Chin

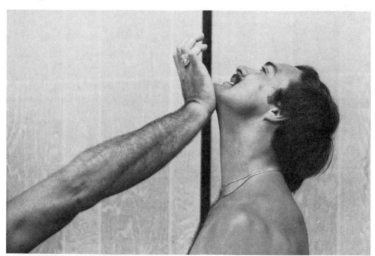

Damage: broken jaw, teeth knocked out, neck snapped back, possible whiplash.
Result: attacker will be knocked out for several minutes, may have broken neck.

Sixty-Three: Palm Heel to Throat

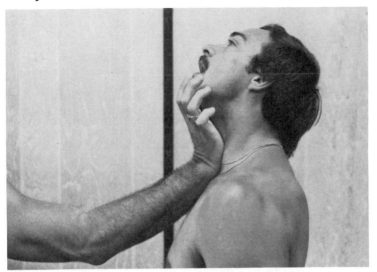

Damage: crushed throat, broken Adam's apple.
Result: attacker will usually die unless given medical help.

Sixty-Four: Palm Heel to Heart

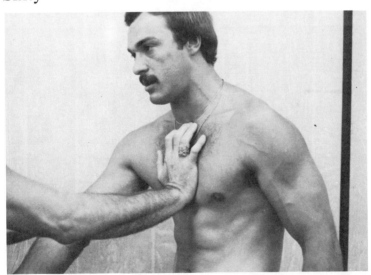

Damage: heart stopped, chest cracked, sternum cracked or broken, possible lung damage.
Result: attacker will be unable to breathe for several minutes, may die.

Sixty-Five: Palm Heel to Temple

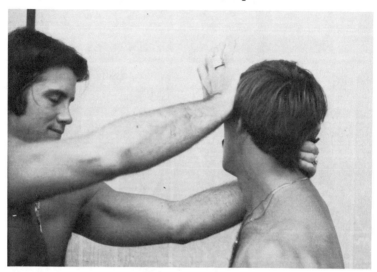

Damage: crushed temple, concussion.
Result: attacker will pass out for several minutes or have a fit.

Sixty-Six: Palm Heel to Back of Head

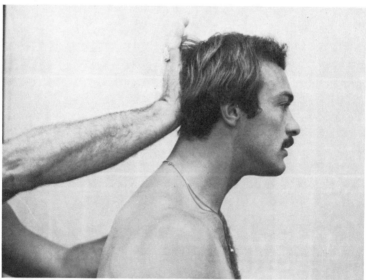

Damage: broken neck, concussion.
Result: attacker will be knocked out, may have permanent crippling or death.

Sixty-Seven: Palm Heel to Kidneys

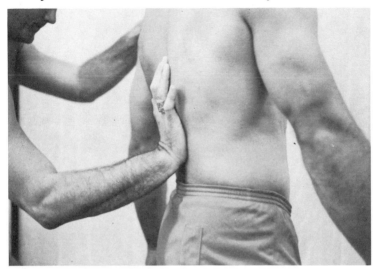

Damage: bruised kidney, broken back.
Result: attacker will fall down, have internal damage.

Sixty-Eight: Elbow to Face

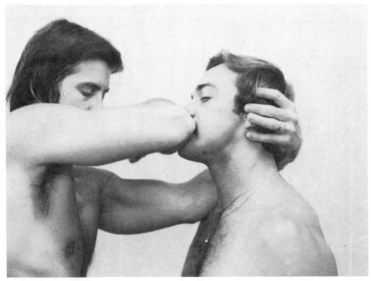

Damage: teeth knocked out, broken jaw, broken nose.
Result: attacker will be knocked out for many minutes; need surgery.

Sixty-Nine: Elbow to Throat

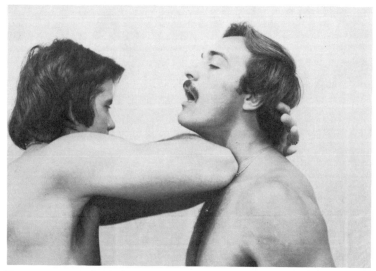

Damage: crushed throat.
Result: death unless given medical attention immediately.

Seventy: Elbow to Point of Chin

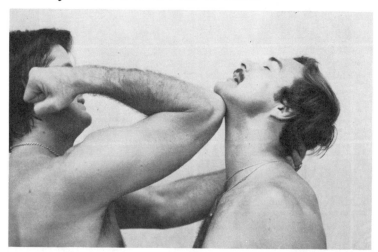

Damage: broken jaw, teeth knocked out, neck snapped back.
Result: attacker will be knocked out, may have broken neck.

Seventy-One: Elbow to Heart—Solar Plexus

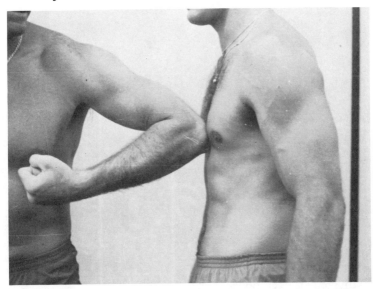

Damage: loss of consciousness, broken chest, stopped heart.
Result: attacker will be unable to breathe for several minutes,
may die.

Seventy-Two: Elbow to Ribs

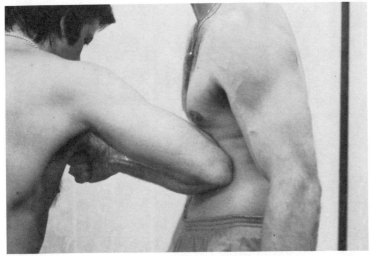

Damage: broken ribs, possible lung damage.
Result: attacker will be unable to breathe for several minutes.

Seventy-Three: Elbow to Groin

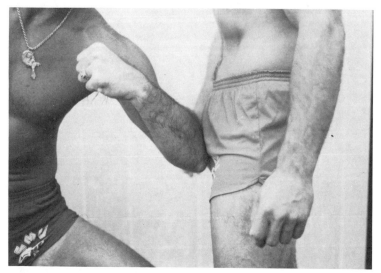

Damage: cracked pelvis, bruised testicles.
Result: attacker will be unable to stand for several minutes, may be crippled.

Seventy-Four: Elbow to Back of Neck

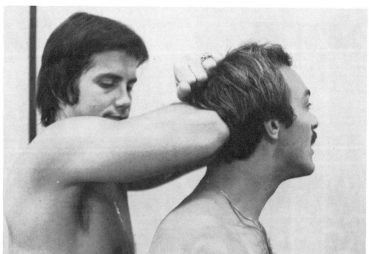

Damage: broken neck.
Result: attacker will be permanently crippled, knocked out; may die.

Seventy-Five: Ridge Hand to Solar Plexus

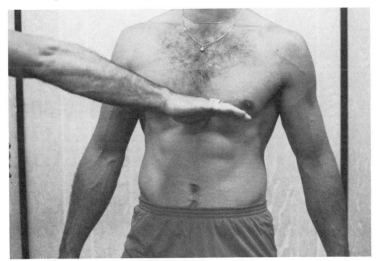

Damage: broken ribs, cracked chest.
Result: attacker will be unable to stand or breathe for several minutes.

Seventy-Six: Ridge Hand to Temple

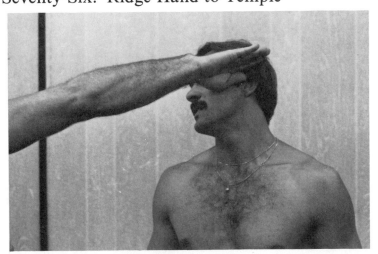

Damage: cracked skull, broken jaw.
Result: attacker will be knocked out or go into a fit.

Seventy-Seven: Ridge Hand to Kidneys

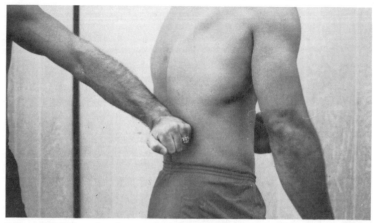

Note: This can be done with the regular ridge hand, or with the bottom fist as shown here, which gives more power, for the ridge hand can be damaging to the thumb if the hand is not trained well.

Damage: bruised kidneys, cracked spine.

Result: kidney damage, extreme pain, death may result.

Seventy-Eight: Ridge Hand to Back of Head

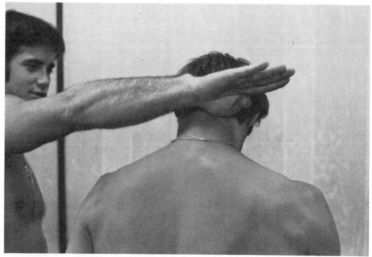

Damage: broken neck.

Result: attacker will be knocked out; may be permanently crippled, may die.

Seventy-Nine: Ridge Hand to Side of Neck

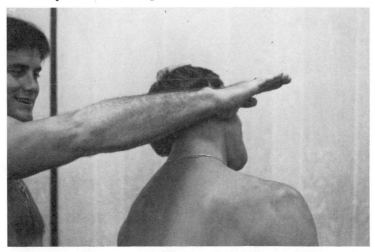

Damage: broken neck, eardrum affected, loss of blood to brain.
Result: attacker will be knocked out for a few minutes.

Eighty: Ridge Hand to Throat

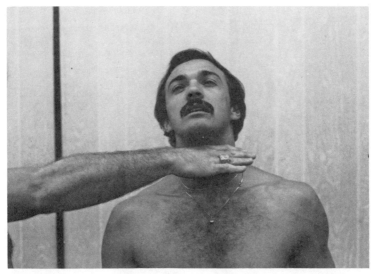

Damage: crushed throat, broken Adam's apple.
Result: attacker will die unless given immediate medical attention.

Eighty-One: Ridge Hand to Bridge of Nose

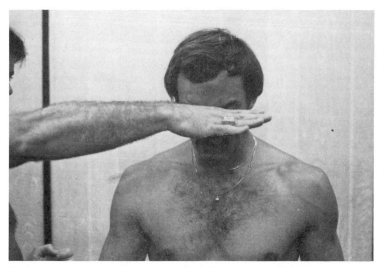

Damage: broken nose, loss of vision, concussion.
Result: attacker will be knocked out for several minutes.

Eighty-Two: Ridge Hand to Groin

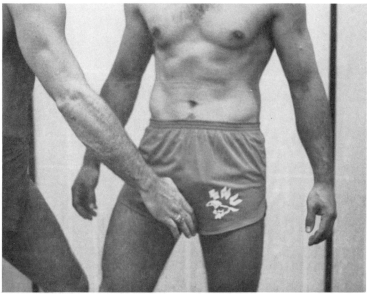

Damage: bruised or crushed testicles, cracked pelvis.
Result: attacker will be unable to stand for several minutes;
may be crippled.

Eighty-Three: Punch to Groin

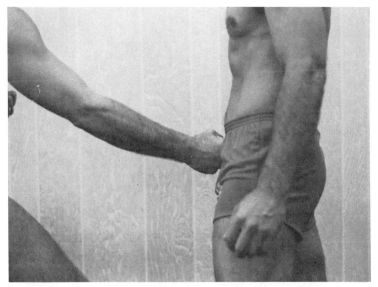

Damage: cracked or broken pelvis, bruised testicles.
Result: attacker will be unable to stand for many minutes;
may be crippled.

Eighty-Four: Punch to Heart

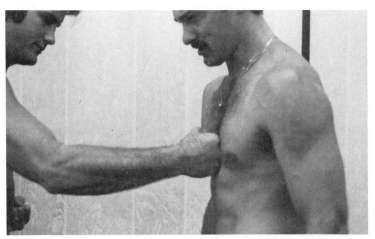

Damage: cracked ribs, cracked sternum, loss of breath, stoppage of heart.
Result: attacker will be unable to breathe for many minutes;
may die.

Eighty-Five: Punch to Throat

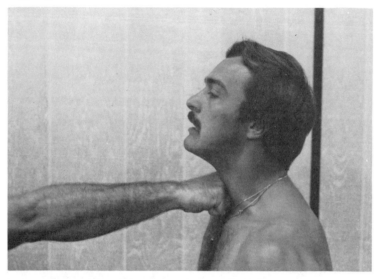

Damage: broken Adam's apple, crushed throat.
Result: attacker will be unable to live unless given medical attention.

Eighty-Six: Punch to Bridge of Nose

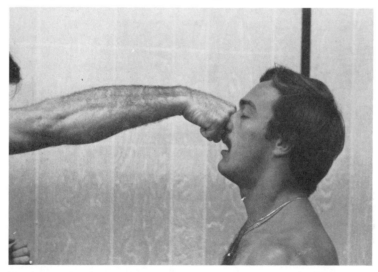

Damage: broken nose, teeth knocked out, eye damage.
Result: attacker will lose consciousness for several minutes or will be unable to see.

Eighty-Seven: Punch to Temple

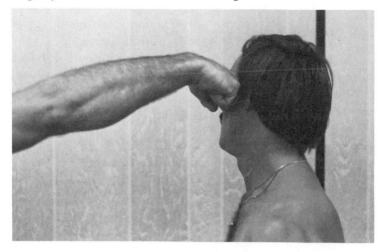

Damage: broken jaw, teeth knocked out, loss of blood to brain.
Result: attacker will be knocked out for many minutes or go into a fit.

Eighty-Eight: Punch to Chin

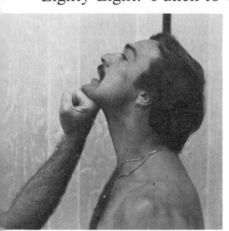

Damage: broken jaw, teeth knocked out.
Result: attacker will be knocked out for several minutes.

Eighty-Nine: Punch to Ribs

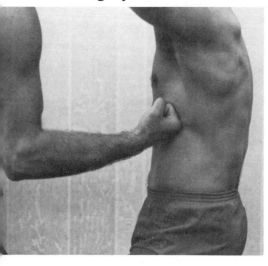

Damage: broken ribs, possible lung damage.
Result: attacker will be unable to breathe for several minutes.

Ninety: Punch to Kidneys

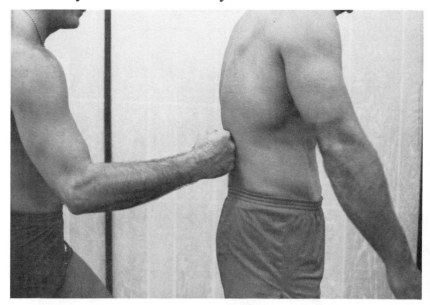

Damage: broken back, bruised kidneys, internal damage.
Result: attacker will fall down, usually have internal damage requiring medical help.

Ninety-One: Punch to Back of Neck

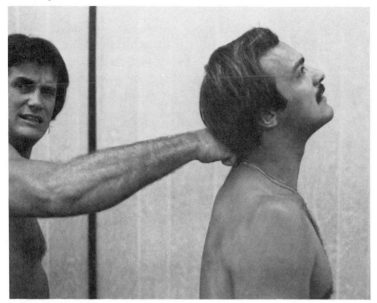

Damage: broken neck.
Result: attacker will be knocked out, usually crippled; may die.

Ninety-Two: Two-Finger Eye Strike

Damage: loss of eyes or scarring of eyes.
Result: attacker will be in great pain, and lose eyesight, perhaps permanently.

Ninety-Three: One-Finger Eye Strike

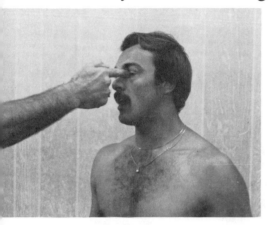

Damage: loss of eye, permanent eye damage.
Result: attacker will lose eye, or will lose sight for a long time.

Ninety-Four: Eye Gouge, Thumb

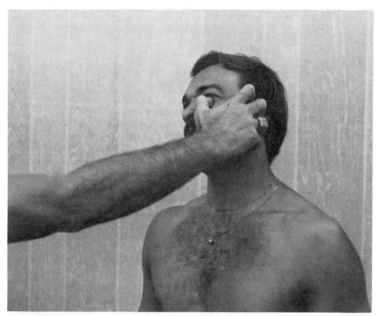

Damage: loss of eye, permanent eye damage.
Result: extreme pain, loss of vision, loss of eye.

Ninety-Five: Double-Eye Gouge

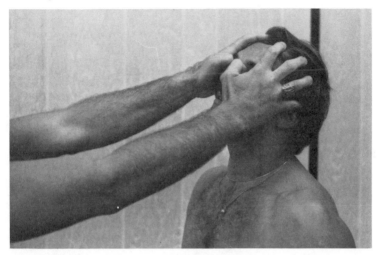

Damage: loss of eyes, loss of vision.
Result: attacker will lose vision, maybe lose eyesight forever.

Ninety-Six: Eardrum Strike

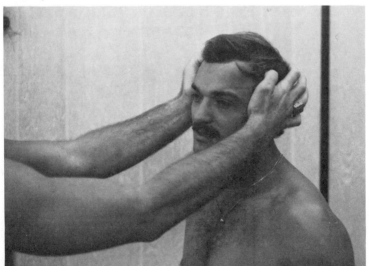

Damage: broken eardrums, cracked jaw.
Result: attacker will be in great pain, lose balance and willingness to fight.

Ninety-Seven: Tiger Claw to Throat

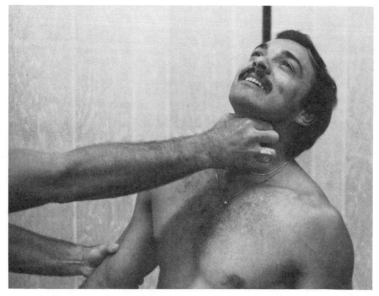

Damage: collapse of larynx.
Result: attacker will die unless pressure is relieved.

Ninety-Eight: Head Butt to the Bridge of Nose

Damage: broken nose, teeth knocked out, cracked skull.
Result: loss of consciousness, internal damage.

Ninety-Nine: Forefinger Strike to Throat

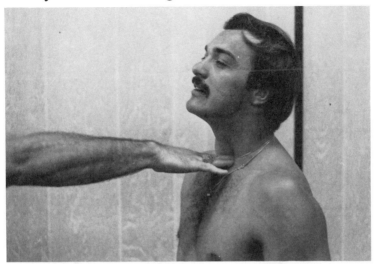

Damage: crushed throat.
Result: attacker will die unless given medical attention.

One Hundred: Two-Handed Strike to Back of Neck

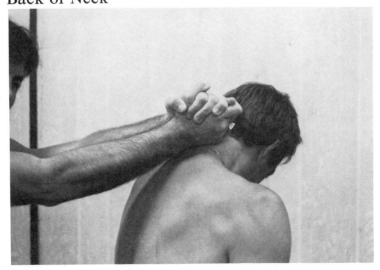

Damage: broken neck.
Result: attacker will be knocked out for many minutes, usually crippled; may die.

5. Street Fighting Applications

The following chapter contains some practical applications for the use of deadly karate blows and kicks in actual street situations. I am not showing all of the techniques you have just learned, but rather I am going to illustrate practical applications of some techniques to get your mind working about how to put techniques together for effective defensive postures. Each situation that you might find yourself involved with in the street can require hundreds of different actions, and all must be done immediately. There is no best technique or action, but you should always try to do what works best for you, after you have practiced all of the techniques.

I do not condone that under any circumstances, short of your imminent death or the impending death of another, that you use these techniques on anyone in the street.

APPLICATIONS

I.   You are standing by your car getting ready to get in when an attacker with a crowbar tries to kill you. You have several courses of action, here are a few: You turn quickly and snap a FRONT KICK into his THROAT.

Before he can reach you, smash his THROAT again with your FIST.

Variation: you can snap a FRONT KICK into his GROIN.

You can snap a SIDE KICK into his CHEST and HEART.

You can snap a BACK KICK into his FACE.

II. You are getting into your car with your wife when two thugs attack you with a crowbar, trying to kill you.

You both react with kicks, the man with a SIDE KICK to the FACE, the woman with a BACK KICK to the GROIN.

You finish them off with STOMPS to the THROAT and NECK.

III. You are walking with your wife when two thugs start to attack you.

The man reacts with a SHUTO to the NECK, the woman with a SNAP KICK to the GROIN.

You finish them off with a STOMP to the GROIN by the man,
and the lady KNEES the FACE of her attacker.

IV.   A lady is walking down
the street when a would-be
rapist grabs her.

She reacts with a ROUND-
HOUSE to the GROIN.

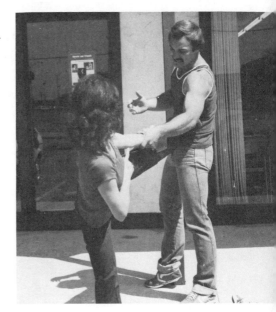

She continues to turn and thrusts a HEEL KICK to the
THROAT, kicking him down where she finishes him with a
STOMP to the HEAD.

V.   You are at the car wash when two men attack you.

You react quickly with a SIDE KICK to the THROAT of one man.

You make a quick PUNCH to the CHIN of the other man.

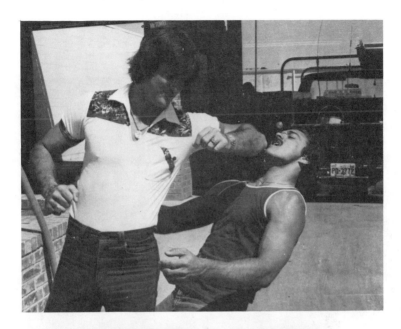

Finish them off with an **ELBOW SMASH** to the **FACE** of one man, and a **STOMP** to the **GROIN** of the other.

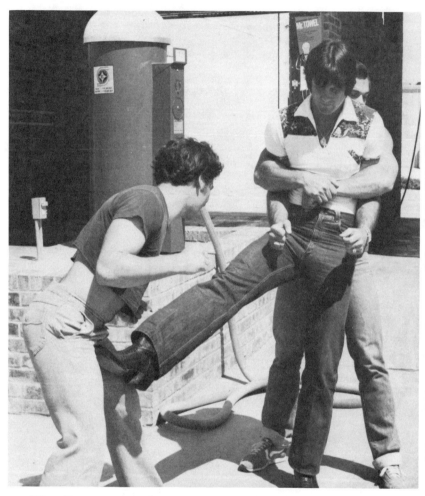

VI. You are at the car wash when two men jump you and manage to grab you. One gets you in a bear hug. You react to the man in front first with a SNAP KICK to the GROIN.

You then do a REAR LIFT KICK to the GROIN of the man holding you.

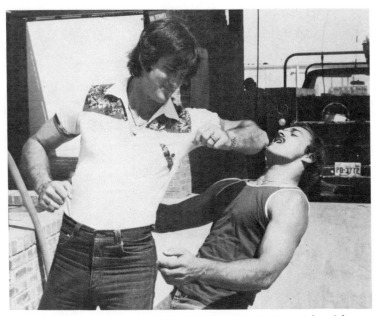

Then come around and SMASH his FACE, knocking him to the ground.

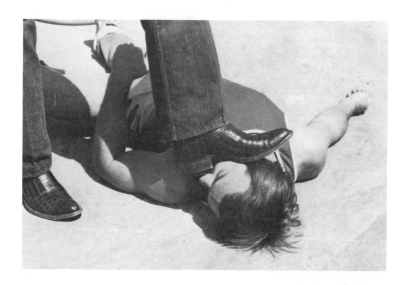

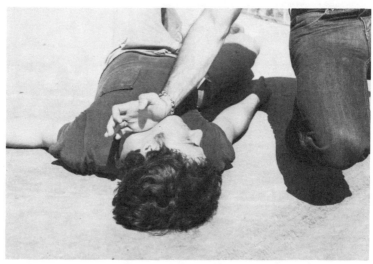

You finish him off with a STOMP to the FACE, and the other with a SHUTO to the THROAT.